Make That Switch

Marvellous Minds. Fabulous Feelings.
Awesome Actions.

PAM WELLI NJAWE

www.MakeThatSwitch.com

MakeThatSwitch071@gmail.com

ISBN: 978-1-9160074-1-3

"Our mind is a garden, our thoughts are the seeds. We can grow flowers or we can grow weeds." Anonymous

---

To every individual who, like me, needs a light turned inward again and again as a reminder of the power within.

Acknowledgements

This book is the product of the Universal presence in and around me, the Source of all things good, beautiful and lovely – thanks to God the Creator of all things.

I offer immense thanks and gratitude to all the people around me who have supported and encouraged me through this process.

To my straight-talking and fun mentors from Business Mastery Live: Nadeem Mohammed, Chan Vekaria and Abz Aneez whose guidance has been spot on! To my writing mate and accountability buddy Bella Tchombe for all the things we shared and learned together and for daring to dream with me.

To Constance Sothern, my editor and proofreader for the unlimited revisions and her warm and collaborative style. To all those who took their time to patiently and lovingly read, re-read and sense check the model for me: Aunty Grace Njopa-Kaba, Jackie Njawe, Harriette Njawe-Wood,

Peter Ashu, Jayne Ekema, Montio Morgan, Venan Sondo, BK Maimo – you all ROCK! Thank you!

Thanks for all words of wisdom freely and happily offered by Dr Satish Chadha and Emma Escott. To my soul sister, Imgard Ekokobe for the gift that set the ball rolling. To all those who provided me with examples from their lives and experiences: Tienche Abena, Ralph Tchombe, Braelan Wood, and others.

And for putting so much meaning into single phrases or sentences that have served as centrepieces throughout this book, I offer deep thanks to all the teachers quoted within these pages.

Contents

Make That Switch - Preface

"Your mind is like a parachute, it only works when it's open" *African Proverb*

Many years ago I sat thinking about my future; what I wanted to do, what I wanted to be. My focus was on my career and I was considering what academic course would lead me into the next phase of my life journey. I wrote three possibilities or more like options on the back page of an old Filofax ☺ with the intention of fulfilling one of the three - I did, in fact, achieve one of them. It was the completion of my Master's degree programme in Public Health. A very long time later, I realised - through repeated experiences - the hidden power in writing my intentions.

Eighteen years later, with a lot of ups and downs and toing and froing, I have learned and experienced enough to fuel my desire to share. My growth is the result of the lessons I have been gifted from God, using channels ranging from friends and family to colleagues and total strangers and from the natural world that surrounds me.

I have learned (and I am still learning) the power that I have in my mind and emotions to bring about the life experiences I desire. This power, that we all possess but were not all taught from childhood, lives within us and is accessible to us at all times. Like every skill, its effective use requires our practice and passion and its results bring forth happiness from within that can withstand the challenges of life.

Now, I live a life that is full of internal happiness and deep appreciation for life. I use the power of focused thought, writing (ingratitude of the present and planning for the future) and inspired action to make my day to day experience of life enjoyable for me and all those I come into contact with. This ultimately is the goal – finding and expressing the state of being that makes life worth living today and every day.

Make That Switch is a simple guide to creating and implementing lasting change in our lives as individuals, and positively impacting on all those around us and who come into contact with us. It leads us into focusing principally on what we want to be, to experience, to feel, to achieve; and takes us away from the downward spiral of looking at, talking about and feeling the unwanted realities of life. This book is not intended to be a quick fix; for some, it will be a reinforcement of what is already being practised; for others an introduction to looking at ourselves in a more positive and nurturing light while for others still, the key to total transformation.

I have shared much of what is in this book with the people who are closest to me in their times of need, and have seen and heard the positive effects of implementing some of these activities. A close friend of mine was finding it really difficult to handle the negative comments from a partner and found that by focusing on the positive aspects and giving them her attention for the majority of the time, those positive aspects became more prominent in her experience, and the negative ones had significantly less of an effect.

It all starts in our minds!

"I make my mind my friend"
Anonymous Samurai poem

Introduction

"Mind is creative..... and all experiences in life are the result of our habitual or predominant mental attitude."

Charles Haanel

The concept of using our minds and emotions to frame and act on our desires, dreams and aspirations in life is recurrent in teachings from centuries ago. Yet the majority of us go through the first decades of our lives ignorant or sometimes dismissive, of these teachings and messages and as a result, we are not able to apply them consistently and effectively to our lives.

The creation of every tool, system, machine, process and other invention in existence today began in the mind of the inventor or innovator. The use of imagination and ingenuity served, and continues to serve, as the precursor to the evolution of our experience of life on this planet. From the manufacturing of crude tools for hunting and farming by early man, through the creation of steam engines and ships, to the advent of social media - tools like Facebook and WhatsApp, the starting point is the same – the mind! I remain utterly fascinated by authors who invent complete other worlds like JK Rowling (the Harry Potter series) to JRR Tolkien (the Lord of the Rings trilogy) and literary fiction writers like Chimamanda Ngozi Adichie (Half of a Yellow Sun). These works began in their minds translated into moving pictures for our entertainment and enthrallment and are examples of what we are *all* capable of – yes, you included! The capability being the art of translation of our thoughts into things and experiences!

Each and every one of us CAN develop this mindset even if we may not necessarily have the tools, knowledge and confidence to implement this in our lives in profitable and sustainable ways. If you have picked up this book, chances are you are ready to take this step for yourself and those people you come into contact with regularly – your family, friends, colleagues and communities.

But it's not just about thinking about your goals and aspirations in a cerebral way. It's about what feelings and emotions you associate with them, what inspired actions you take towards their achievement, how you sustain those actions and keep the momentum when you face challenges and obstacles and how you utilise internal and external resources to your advantage. It's not about turning a blind eye to problems, or burying your head in the sand when faced with challenges. It's about acknowledging them but focusing much more attention, much more emotion and all the inspired action into the solution, the vision, and the good bits of the road ahead. It is possible to stay grounded but stand tall enough to have your head in the clouds!

Prayer

"Ask, and it shall be given to you; seek, and you shall find; knock, and it shall be opened to you. For everyone who asks receives, and he who seeks finds, and to him who knocks it shall be opened." Matthew 7: 7-8

In her Super Soul Sunday interviews, Oprah Winfrey usually ends concludes by asking the guests their definition of words like *love*, *prayer* and *the soul*. Those questions always got me thinking and I would answer them for myself and often give a different answer each time.

Here I have the chance to give my full answer to the question "what is prayer to me?" and I can make it as long as I wish (Oprah, please note ☺).

I see prayer as what we do all the time and throughout the day in our lives. Whether deliberately considered as such or not, whether directed to self or others, prayer to me is

A thought, a vision, a feeling

A question, a word, a wish

An action, an intention

An appreciation, an affirmation

I see my life as a continuous prayer and therefore this book, with all its activities, is a prayer and my service to you.

In any case and for every form of what I call prayer, the root of its effectiveness is clearly resident in faith.

"….all things for which you pray and ask, believe that

you have received them, and they shall be granted you."

Mark 11:24

This book uses examples from real people, ordinary people who have applied the right mindset to situations in their lives and witnessed the unfolding of those desires. It provides practical suggestions that you can apply to every area of your life, and as with most things in life, the extent of your application is proportional to the extent of your resulting experience. The mental attitude it seeks to promote is solution-focused: can do, will-happen and must-happen; whilst recognising, appreciating, learning from and enjoying every step of the journey.

It is not expected that this is read in one sitting – oh no! There are two very important factors to consider when using this book to enhance and embed your learning: writing things down as you go (and we'll cover this further) and sharing the things you learn, discover or see in a new light with those close to you. So basically, take your time to read, digest, plan, write and share. Writing things that you want, learn or aspire to, has a way of focusing the mind unlike any other and gives you a reference to go back to down the line. It provides positive reinforcement for you to continue to apply these methods and provides evidence to share with others. Sharing your learning with others also enables you to enrich the experience of those people and further reinforces your own learning and experience. Sharing indeed is caring – for all involved!

Make That Switch – The Model

"You only have control over three things in your life – the thoughts you think, the images you visualise, and the actions you take." *Jack Canfield*

The model for *Make That Switch* is simple and brings together a combination of teachings and messages from a broad range of authors and speakers; personal experiences from my life and those of close friends and family. Throughout my adult life I have had timely conversations, listened to audio messages, read books and had experiences that have each been the foundations to the next step on my journey of growth and development. This book reflects those experiences in a structured way and includes practical tips to give them meaning and purpose in your life.

The benefit of using a rich array of sources can be likened to the viewing of a large mural in a darkened room with narrow-beam flashlights by a large group of people. Each person has a flashlight with a view of the mural based on where they are standing and where they are pointing their flashlights; and the collective stories of their views and experiences enables the reader to begin to put together the full image of the mural. Our individual life stories, experiences and perceptions uniting to enrich the shared message we deliver.

The four stages or 'seasons' of this model are Realisation, Visualisation, Inspired Action and Reinforcement. There will be positive, constructive and growth-focused questions to help clarify your thoughts and intentions during each stage and these examples will be listed for you to consider as you progress through the seasons and episodes.

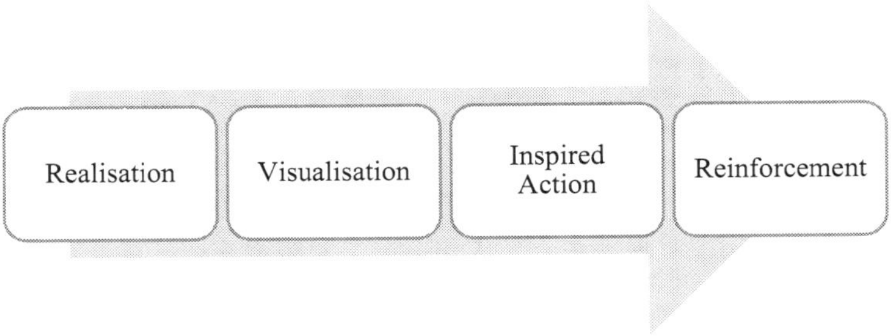

Realisation | Visualisation | Inspired Action | Reinforcement

The events we encounter in our everyday lives, both good and not-so-good, are a continual source for renewal for all the stages. We are continually examining and assessing our current situation in different areas of our lives and realising what we would prefer; which leads us to creating and modifying our desires and dreams for ourselves and then inspiring us to new actions. We can view every negative experience or situation as an opportunity to improve, and taking these steps provides the framework that enables us to do so.

Realisation

This stage sets the foundation by allowing us to examine the current situation and circumstance in an area of our lives that we would like to change. It provides a method for us to consider the pillars that support those unwanted experiences or situations, and our ability to make the necessary changes to replace those pillars with new ones more aligned to the life we desire. We begin to understand and apply the underlying activities that will initiate the whole process.

Visualisation

This stage offers some suggestions on how to define, sharpen and clarify our positive image, and describes the importance of our emotional connection to that image. The activities guide us through the practical application of these suggestions.

Inspired Action

This stage helps us identify those actions that are feasible and practical and hold the potential to be sustainable. It provides some suggestions on how to ensure we hold ourselves to account for undertaking the actions and utilise our close networks to support us.

Reinforcement

This stage is all about ensuring there is resilience in our plans to meet our goals/targets. How do we handle periods when motivation is low or when obstacles seem insurmountable? Here we will have some activities we should all have in reserve to pull out in those times when we need to refocus, recharge and keep going!

Working through the 'seasons' and 'episodes'

Like every great television series, this book will take you through 'seasons' for each stage and 'episodes' for each activity. It is phased in a progressive and hopefully fun way! You will have some work to do within each episode as any actor would, but don't worry; there'll be clear guidance on how to do that. Remember – YOU are the lead actor/actress in this series and this is YOUR script! So enjoy it!

Make That Switch – Season 1, 'Realisation'

"You must learn a new way to think before you can master a new way to be."
Marianne Williamson

There comes a point in most people's lives where the need to do or experience things differently springs out of nowhere and manifests as a voice in our heads, starting as the occasional nudge or whisper, and gradually getting louder and louder until we either find a way to put a muzzle on it or succumb to its calling. This voice can be the result of a positive or negative experience we go through like acquisitions or loss (people, jobs, finances, etc.), or just from the need to inject more purpose, passion, excitement or joy into our life experiences.

In some cases, something stops us in our tracks. Doubts about ourselves and abilities to achieve those desires and visions of our lives begin to creep in, and before we know it, we've talked ourselves out of them. We somehow dig out and find the one or two things that would make achieving that goal 'too difficult', 'unreasonable', 'unfeasible' or 'impossible'. We find ways to stay in our comfort zones and convince ourselves our dreams are too far-fetched.

Well, let me tell you a story about...... my rose plant!

I had a rose plant in my garden for about 10 years before a home extension project saw it uprooted. It was a beautiful plant that bloomed with pinkish white roses every summer. It had two main branches that grew to about 5 feet tall in the summer months. I was never really good at maintaining plants back then so didn't really nurture it properly. As a result, it developed a plant infestation at which point I did try to help with the recommended treatment and the result was good. I learnt to prune it at the beginning of winter but it struggled during the next summer.

Now, here is the interesting part. The following summer, the rose plant budded a new branch, as if to say "you've ignored me long enough - I can look after myself!" It hadn't done that for years. This new branch came up directly from the main trunk and to make things more surprising for me, it grew to over 6 feet tall! The old branches stopped growing completely in this process, as if the plant was channelling all of its energy and focus into the new, tall, healthy one.

Now why did I just make you read that? What did I learn from the plant that makes it relevant to the topic of realisation? I learned a few things from this simple occurrence in nature, which is probably no surprise to rose experts.

1. It's never too late to make a change in your life.
2. Your 'old self' can stop growing to make room for the new you.
3. Recognising and responding to the call to express your talents and gifts leads you to soar higher than you ever have.

4. The new you comes from within yourself.

This story is summed up quite nicely in this statement by Ray Stanford as quoted by Bob Proctor: “If you don’t like the results you are getting in your life, you’re going to have to change YOU because they are YOUR results.”

So now, all you new-branch-budding rose plants, let’s get started with our activities!

Alert: you may need a few things as an actor within this production, so perhaps a trip to the shops is in order right about now. On your list please include post-it notes (if you like bright colours and/or different shapes, go for it!), pens or pencils of your choice, either a noticeboard to pin things on or a whiteboard to write directly on.

Episode 1.1 – Using questions as the gateway into your new mindset

> ***"Successful people ask better questions, and as a result, they get better results." Tony Robbins***

Providing an answer to an existing question can be very rewarding, but asking a new and powerful question can open up a brand new chapter in our lives. Earlier I mentioned constructive and growth-focused questions that would form part of each stage. Now it's time to list and answer a few such questions and in addition write some of yours down – and yes, you can ask additional ones and write them in the table below. Begin by identifying the area of your life where you would like to see a change. It could be to improve your health and fitness - like a desire to lose weight or improve strength and flexibility in your body; improve your mental health and resilience; improve your performance in your current job or develop the skill set to get a new one. It could be developing an effective strategy to cope with or manage a chronic problem.

These questions are more constructive and powerful when they are geared towards the future you want and not based on explaining or dwelling on problems in the present or past. So questions like 'why has this happened?' may just limit our focus on the problem, blinding us to other possibilities. Questions like those listed below help to formulate the plans to achieve a more positive focus, and therefore a more positive outcome.

Questions	**Your answers**
What area(s) of my life do I need to develop a more positive and focused mindset?	For example, weight loss, new job, financial earnings, etc
What current thoughts and feelings do I need to replace?	For example, "I'm fat", "I'm broke", etc
What self-beliefs do I need to recognise, nurture and portray?	
What would it take to realise that I am worthy of a good life?	
How can I express the best of myself in everything I do?	

The last two questions listed above will hopefully give you an opportunity to explore your personal potential. To change the way you think often requires a change in your opinion about yourself. Not the way you portray yourself, but the fundamental opinion you hold about you as a being. My hope is that you (and I) are continuously growing into the fullness of our potential in life. To that end, you'll find a question to provide food for thought at the end of each season – I'll call it the BEST ME check. You can use that question to pause and consider your bigger picture.

The concept of BEST Me is rooted in the values that we hold as good and true for ourselves and that we aspire to being. Not simply portraying but actually embodying. To me, Maslow's hierarchy of needs is all about attaining the best version of ourselves through self-actualisation. To get there we go through fulfilling our need to belong and our need to build self-esteem. Hopefully this book will give you the tools to do this.

At this stage, I hope the powerful and purpose-driven questions you have written down and the corresponding answers are already making you feel more empowered and are beginning to build your enthusiasm. These answers (which can expand every time you revisit the question) will provide a springboard to forming and sharpening your ideal positive image, which we will look into in the next season.

Episode 1.2 – Expressing gratitude

"The real voyage of discovery consists not in seeing new landscapes, but in having new eyes." *Marcel Proust*

So you've identified what areas you want to work on and examined your current mindset and emotions that you want to change. Take a pause now and give some thought to the things that are going well in your life. A well-known author and life coach, Tony Robbins, once stated that when we are grateful and are feeling that gratitude, we can't be anxious or stressed at the same time. When we need to find and express good emotions in our everyday lives, we often turn to these things quite naturally. We think of the people in our lives, the environment we live in, and the places we've been to amongst other things. We can be good at acknowledging them but this activity goes one step further. You've guessed it – write them down!

Throughout this process, I would suggest a new habit for your daily routine if you don't already do this. This is the daily habit of keeping a gratitude journal! You may be thinking that you are already grateful and thankful and appreciative of all the good things in your life so what is the use of writing things down? This brings us back to the reinforcing power of writing mentioned earlier on. Writing makes things more tangible, more vivid and in the case of gratitude, provides a current focus and future source of inspiration for yourself (as you'll see later) and anyone you care to share it with. It is said that whatever we focus on expands in our experience of it, so in that light, if we want more things to be grateful for, then we must focus on those things we are grateful for now.

Don't simply count your blessings; record them

In addition, just knowing that you will be doing this everyday makes you more conscious of the need to look for things to be appreciative of and thankful for. As you get more and more into writing these things down, you may even find yourself looking for the positive in not-so-positive situations just to have more to write about. And we are talking about everything about your day and life: your natural surroundings, physical body, characteristics in yourself and others and even the economy!

So, let's start off with a plan to write at least three things each day beginning with one or more of these phrases:

I am thankful for……..

I appreciate or am appreciative of ………..

I liked ……..

To deepen this practice further and relive the emotion of the thing you are appreciating, add two 'whys' for every item. So for instance, "I am thankful for my friend who took time to listen to me explain an issue because it made me feel heard and allowed me to see the issue more clearly." This is a technique used and taught by the Neuro-Linguistic Programme trainer, Satish Chadha. I found it helps me relive the emotion of whatever I am appreciating as I write, which could be hours afterwards.

I learnt a really good way to embed a new habit about a year into the start of recording my items of appreciation. I wasn't very consistent until I teamed up with a good friend who suggested we make each other accountable for recording our blessings on a daily basis for thirty days. So every day we would write our lists at whatever time and format we chose, but in addition we would share some or all of them in a message to each other. This happened every day for the agreed thirty day period, and although I have missed the odd day here and there, my recording practice has remained strong ever since.

Sharing in this way gave both of us ideas of the types of things to include in our individual lists, and made us more aware of those things that we would not have necessarily considered. Depending on the habit , opinions on how long it takes to embed vary widely: some say 21 days and others up to 66 days.

So with this activity, and based purely on my experience, set an intention of writing down at least three items a day for a period of 30 days. If it helps to buddy up, please do. And then keep going!

Episode 1.3 – Affirmations to reveal the soul

> ***"It's the repetition of affirmations that leads to belief. And once that belief becomes deep conviction, things begin to happen." Muhammad Ali***

We've all received compliments at some point or other in our lives from other people. We can generally sense when they are sincere and understand the role they can have in reinforcing the good/ desirable aspects of ourselves. This behaviour of paying compliments is learned and many of us (dare I say, all of us?) use it to let those around us know what we like, what we admire and what we would like them to do and be more of.

For some reason, there isn't the same enthusiasm to self-affirm. I don't know about you, but I always thought there was something arrogant about self-affirming. It was as if, someone else had to see the good quality in me for it to be true. If I saw it in myself, I was delusional but if another saw it, it must be objective and therefore true.

So this activity is about learning to self-affirm to support the development of a positive mindset. For some, this might be quite simple in that you may already have a list of positive affirmations you use regularly. For others, this might be totally new, and not easy; so my suggestion would be to start with the compliments you have received that you can identify with. If possible, pick a compliment that you can internalise and attribute to your core inner self.

For instance, someone may have said to you: "you are really good at giving care and attention to detail in undertaking tasks." You can internalise that into "I am caring and attentive" and in so doing, realise that the attribute can apply to any other area in your life you direct it to.

It's writing time, so make a note of one or two affirmations on the post-it notes or one of your boards and put them somewhere noticeable so you'll see them every day – like your fridge, bathroom mirror, bedroom wall opposite your bed or in your car! They might include phrases like:

- I am able and capable
- I am solution-focused
- I am happy

And finally, don't forget to share, share, share!

BEST ME CHECK!

After completing the activities in season 1, do I recognise the emergence of the BEST ME in the area I have chosen to change?

Make That Switch – Season 2, 'Visualisation'

> ***"We have within each of us the power to make ourselves whatever we wish to be."***
> ***David Baird***

The use of visualisation in this model is not limited to the mental image of the desired outcome, it relates to a combination of what we see for ourselves, how closely we identify with that vision and how strongly we feel about it. This level of clarity comes to us when we can answer the type of questions that explore the very nature of our desires and enables us to make firm DECISIONS about our intentions.

It might be useful to look back at something in your life that you achieved, even though it appeared difficult or even impossible at the start, and whether it was big or small. What were the ingredients that made it happen? Would you include any of these?

- ✓ You were very clear about what you wanted – you made a DECISION.
- ✓ You just had to have it/do it/ experience it – it was a must happen.
- ✓ You could see it in your mind and really FEEL it too.
- ✓ Every time you thought of it, the positive feeling came flooding back and reinforced all of the points above.
- ✓ Any doubt you may have had was smaller in magnitude compared to the passion and determination to achieve it.

If you did include one or more of these as the ingredients to the success of past ventures, then you recognise that you had clarity, determination, passion and focus.

Episode 2.1 – Positive ideal image

"In order to carry a positive action we must develop here a positive vision." Dalai Lama

So you've identified the area in your life you want to make a change in, the negative emotions you no longer wish to entertain and the areas in your life that you are thankful for.

Now it's time to look at the next set of questions to develop that image of the experience you want for yourself.

Here are some suggestions:

Questions	***Your answers***
What new image do I want for myself in my chosen area of change?	
How specific can I be in my definition?	

The question about being specific is a significant addition to the 'what', as it gives meaning to our image and facilitates the clarity of the desired outcome.

It also leads us to make a decision. There is something so powerful and definite about making a decision. *It's like the sound of a gavel – everything is brought to order within our minds and we get a sense of resolve to turn our full attention to an intention.*

I have experienced an almost tangible difference in my life when I moved from sitting on the fence and shunning the driving seat to taking full responsibility for my life and making firm decisions. This was most obvious in the move from having all my decisions made for me by parents or parent-figures to realising the need to do this myself. This may sound simple but if you were not taught decision-making and its importance, this is actually quite a big step.

The process of developing the image may be a straightforward answer - like being a few sizes smaller (and defining the end size or weight), having a stronger body or having optimal blood pressure or blood sugar levels (again defined quantitatively). In such cases, it is relatively easier to define and be clear about the intended outcome. But what if you can't even see this positive image or you can't achieve the clarity you would love to have?

There are a few things you may want to consider to help you build the image to focus on and this includes looking to things and people that inspire you in those areas. But before we go into that, consider this: having a strong idea of what you don't want provides a good place to start formulating an idea of what you do want. In some cases it is a matter of defining the opposite of the thing you don't want. If we don't want unhappiness, our ideal image is to be happy; if we don't want to be in debt, our ideal image may be abundance.

Getting ideas from our role models can help us make the choices about what we want and what is important for us to experience and/or achieve. Furthermore, stepping outside our usual environment can lead to new ideas, ways of thinking and potential experiences that can inspire a new vision for ourselves.

This act of stepping outside our usual routine and environment might be a very small change, like walking or driving via a different route to work, sitting somewhere different during lunch and talking to new people or attending talks, seminars or classes to adopt new skills and hobbies. For me, going for walks, attending seminars and workshops and watching online videos that motivate and inspire me have been the most productive sources of new ideas.

It is worth noting that our image can be a direction as well as a goal. When I decided to take a regular yoga class, I did not have any specific end in mind. The direction of travel was, however, quite clear: enjoy the process and the physical improvements in my body and see how far I could go. It was later down the line that I started to set specific goals in terms of which postures I would like to achieve and how much strength and flexibility I was working towards.

So now you have that positive vision and have made a decision about it, it's time to write it down. But let's get a little creative with the writing this time to make this image clear and exciting. Start by writing it on a post-it note and/or on your board of choice, and then add a pictorial image to really bring it to life. It's up to you how you set up this picture and any of these options would do (you could even think of more!). The only condition is, it must give you daily access to the image without too much reliance on your memory to seek it out.

Printed picture on your board, fridge, or elsewhere in your home or office

Screensaver on phone or other device (iPad, laptop)

Household or office item with an image representing your vision from a shop (like a mug or calendar)

Taped picture or statement on your gym bag or water bottle

Episode 2.2 – Tweaking the lens for clarity

> ***"Clarity is power. The more clear you are about what you want the more likely you are to achieve it."*** *Billy Cox*

A lot of the time, we set aims and goals for ourselves that we are unable to achieve because they are not clear enough and this ends up causing frustration as we continue to struggle to reach them. What we want is to gain clarity that makes our goals (or the main aspect of the goal) as clear as our knowledge that the sun is brightly shining above the clouds on a grey and rainy day. Clarity can strengthen and be strengthened by your faith in the actualisation of the goal.

Clarity provides the unwavering and unshakeable pillars upon which our inspired actions build our goals. Sometimes, the process of painting for ourselves this clear and focused picture of our positive image can take a little time, but it is well worth the time.

There is a very powerful question that could lead to more clarity and added momentum for you at this stage. The question is simply 'why?' *WHY* can open our minds up to new possibilities by making us think outside the box and not follow any other person's ideas of what our lives should look like.

Why do I want that positive image that I hold? How will it benefit me and those around me, in my family, my community and society as a whole? This question can be the key to the clarity you need to hold onto and to maintain your positive image; as well as determine the degree of emotional connection to it that will see you through to achievement. The answer to this question can help you regain your focus when you encounter difficulties and obstacles on the way. The more compelling the answer to the question, the stronger the intention and this, in turn, results in a deeper emotional connection to reaching the goal.

Remember this quote when it comes to achieving clarity:

> ***"Clarity is your mind's natural state."*** *Jamie Smart*

Giving yourself the time and space to hear the answers you seek from within yourself is a very good way to achieve clarity. Jamie Smart's book on clarity really goes into this concept in depth and likens achieving clarity of mind to allowing mud in a clouded pond to settle. When the mind is clear, the way forward is revealed.

For this activity, consider the questions below and as before add a few (or a lot!) of your own. Then give yourself some time and space to sit in silence or in meditation to declutter your mind and allow your deep self to show you the way and provide the answers.

Questions	*Your answers*
Why do I want that positive image that I hold?	
How will it benefit me and those around me, in my family, community and society?	

Behind the scenes tip on positive images and clarity

Have you ever had the experience of shopping for groceries when you are hungry? I have and so have quite a few people I have spoken to. When I have done it, and especially without a definite shopping list (and sometimes despite the list!), I have made the most inappropriate and unusual choices of food. They have all been about satisfying the current and dominant symptom – hunger.

That's similar when it comes to making a decision, setting a goal or seeking clarity from a place of negative thought or emotion. Tony Robbins encourages us to make decisions from a place of passion and that way our decisions are more in line with our fundamental selves and principles and hold more promise of achievement.

The role of Emotions

> ***"Your emotions affect every cell in your body. Mind and body, mental and physical, are intertwined." Thomas Tutko***

Emotions form a very important part of our lives. When we think about what we want in our lives and the goals we pursue, ultimately it is because we believe they will give us a positive emotional outcome - be it joy, happiness, peace, contentment or a host of others.

The challenge is often in the fact that the current circumstance or experience we are focusing our thoughts on, can lead us into emotions that are not necessarily positive, and our ability to replace the negative emotions with positive ones is not as easy as flicking on a light switch. But we are here to *Make That Switch*, so let's look at one of a few techniques.

Emotions can be graded along a continuum: from hopelessness and despair through to joy and peace, with numerous emotions in between. Depending on where we are at any given time or in any area of our lives and where we want to be, the 'distance' we need to travel to achieve the highest emotions can look and feel insurmountable.

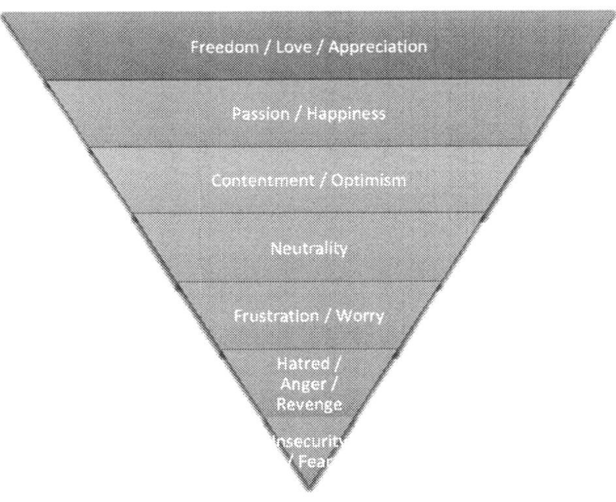

Based on the Abraham Hicks Emotional Scale (from the book Ask and it is Given)

In practical terms, going from fear to freedom or even optimism can be difficult if the expectation is to do it in one fell swoop. Giving yourself a positive ideal image can help you move from one level to the next in sequence and is one way to work up the scale. Another, sometimes easier way, is to move to a place of neutrality and that is where the practice of mindfulness (and meditation) comes in. From a place of neutrality or neutral emotion, it is much easier to build ourselves up to the emotion of our ideal positive image.

How mindfulness can enhance positive emotional transitions

> ***"Who looks outside, dreams;***
> ***who looks inside, awakes."***
> ***Carl Jung***

One of the many definitions of mindfulness is:

"a mental state achieved by focusing one's awareness on the present moment, while calmly acknowledging and accepting one's feelings, thoughts and bodily sensations…" (online dictionary)

This is often described as being *in the now*. Paying attention to whatever is going on in the moment, without judgement. For some, it can be a daily routine with time set aside at any time in the day, or for others, it can be a conscious and purposeful reaction when we face negative emotion – a sort of self-imposed time out. It can be a walk in the park or other activity that provides inspiration or calm.

Episode 2.3 – Positive emotional connection

> ***"Your thoughts affect your emotions. Your emotions affect your decisions. Your decisions affect your life."***
> ***Anonymous***

Earlier on, I touched on the importance of the emotional connection we have to our vision as an ingredient to achieving the desired outcome. Here, we will convert that into an activity to enable you to tap into and utilise your emotions to give added momentum to your vision. Our thoughts and emotions are inextricably linked in that our emotions are the product of our thoughts in a very direct way. Consider these examples:

- ✓ We think about our favourite team playing a competitive game and feel the elation of a win just by imagining it.

- ✓ We can experience the frustration of not completing a work project as deadlines loom.
- ✓ We get tearful thinking about a sad time in our lives or watching tragedies in the lives of others.
- ✓ We feel passionate when we visualise ourselves in our ideal positive image.

By giving these things (or others that you can think of) some focused thought, I am sure you realise that your emotions followed them; and with continued focused on the thought, the emotions grew, and sometimes exponentially.

The fact that some of these situations may not be current or even real, as is the case when we consider the fictional stories we were told as children, the films we watch or the theoretical debates we engage in, often does not prevent or stem the emotional response we experience.

In episode 1.1, you identified the thoughts and feelings that you consider undesirable and wish to replace with more positive ones. Those negative feelings are the ones associated with the current situation you want to change, or better still, that you *are* in the process of changing. We normally simply throw out anything we no longer want, like old clothes and damaged possessions, so instinctively, there may be a temptation to try doing the same with emotions and actively fight against them to push them out of our minds and hearts. While this may seem like a logical way to get rid of them, the experience of most is that the more you resist and fight against them, the more you are aware of them and therefore experiencing them. A simple analogy here would be trying to get rid of darkness in a room by pushing it out a window instead of simply switching on a light! So the more effective method is to develop the positive thoughts and hence emotions in order to *replace* the undesired ones.

Question

What feelings would I experience at the point of achieving the goals and ambitions as set out in my ideal positive image?

For the next activity, make a list of the positive emotions that you have identified as being related to the ideal positive image you created as per the question above. Again, write down each emotion on a separate post-it note and put them up in as many places as you can within your home and even at work - if it helps, make them colourful and include emoticons if you wish!

Remember! These are the emotions you expect to feel if you had the outcome you are aiming for in your positive ideal image. There is no limit (lower or upper) to the number of emotions you can write down. Whether it's one or twenty, the daily reminder here will help you practice and reinforce both the thought and the emotion itself.

Example from a student of happiness

About a year ago, a good friend sent me a message complimenting a picture of me he had seen. His comment was that I looked happy and confirmation that I was happy led to questions and guesses as to what material things could have produced said happiness. Was it a new job or relationship? But my response wasn't what he expected; I had *chosen* to be happy (an emotion linked to all my goals) and consciously looked for internal and external reasons to *be* happy. The late Wayne Dyer used to say to himself at the beginning of the day and I paraphrase, "today is my day and I won't let anyone or anything spoil it for me". The intention to control our emotions using gratitude and positive emotional connections to our goals is a good place to start. I now have 'be happy' on my wardrobe, and it does make me smile.

Example from determined man with diabetes

MD was diagnosed with diabetes over 20 years ago in adulthood and had been on insulin from the start. The side effects had so far been unpleasant in terms of weight gain especially, and he had been unable to lose weight for a long time. He set himself the goal of losing weight and made the decision to stop insulin and that became the basis for his inspired actions. Despite being advised against this decision by the health professionals supporting him, he maintained his focus, was extremely clear about what he wanted and why, and did not allow himself or anyone else to derail him. He went on to stop insulin, lost all the weight he had put on and is now able to manage his condition without the unwanted side effects.

Episode 2.4 – Setting time frames

> ***"A time frame is an essential part of goal setting, because it helps you commit and increases your focus." Ted Robbins***

Giving thought and consideration to *when* you want to achieve your goal is the main point of this episode. At this point your ideal image is clear and you feel an emotional connection to it that has added to the momentum you have built in undertaking the activities so far. The added benefit of giving yourself a time frame is like adding fuel to your engine, strengthening your resolve and commitment; and this supports the next step which is planning the actions inspired by your positive ideal image.

In some cases, setting time frames can be relatively easy because your goal might have been set based on a predetermined target date from the start. For instance, the need to lose weight to attend a significant occasion or event, or the need to complete a course of study to sit an exam, are both goals that already have clear time frames. If there is such an occasion or event that can provide the target date to aim for, then by all means use it. Those time frames in themselves can hold you to account, and you might find it useful to count down the days using a calendar (if that provides you with positive momentum).

I have found that if there is no such predetermined time frame, it helps to create one for yourself. The potential problem of not setting a target date is the possibility of the actions being set too loosely and the goal just moving further and further away into the horizon of time. As an example, let me share my experience of writing this book. I started it on 6th June 2018 with a plan to have a first draft by the end of July and by my original estimation the book would be about 10,000 words long. By the end of July, I had written just over 8,500 words and was very pleased with my rapid progress especially considering the fact that I did the vast majority of the work on Sundays. That time frame worked but what happened next was I didn't set a similar date for completion.

As I wrote out this episode, I realised that and made a snap decision. I had to get this book ready for publication by Christmas!

So now back to our activity. When do YOU want to see this goal come to fruition? My suggestion would be to set it not too soon where you could give up under the pressure of a tight deadline, but not so far that you'll take your foot off the pedal on the actions. If you need to talk to someone about the time frame then do so.

I would also suggest you set some quick win time frames. You may have an ultimate one, but it helps boost your achievement if you decide what you want to have achieved within one week (and weekly after that), then within a month and then regularly from then on. Passion and urgency are a sweet cocktail for reaching goals! So start with a one week target to get the ball rolling. As you celebrate the small wins every week, your confidence soars!

When you have decided on the time frame and date for completion, go ahead and write it down next to your ideal positive image and experience the exhilaration of having a date when you intend to be celebrating the achievement you have set. Underneath that, write your short term goals and time frames – remember to start with one week!

Behind the scenes tip on time frames

Later on we will look at the importance of having an accountability buddy when we have decided and defined our inspired actions. But here I want to mention the benefits of having a mentor or coach as we work towards our goals. I mention this as a tip because it may not apply to all situations. A coach or mentor can help work through your needs and support you with tools to help set goals. More importantly, they can hold you to account in a more formal way and that can result in better results quicker.

Visual prompts

Now you have defined the ideal positive image, identified the emotions related to your image and put these two things in written and image forms on post-it notes, whiteboard or noticeboard. It's time to review them and if needed, move things around a little so that each and every day you have sight of all or at least most of them. By this quite simple exercise, you have converted your dreams and desires into decisions and intentions!

BEST ME CHECK!

How is the BEST ME reflected in my clear positive image and emotional connection?

Make That Switch – Season 3, 'Inspired Action'

> ***"Your positive action combined with positive thinking results in success."***
> *Shiv Khera*

The actions that we take towards the fulfilment of our desires, when we are clear in our focus and are emotionally connected to our goals, can be (and generally are) inspired and proactive rather than forced and reactive. Because of the positive emotional connection to the outcome, inspired actions feel less stressful and provide a pull towards the target rather than a push away from the current circumstance. The push is forced and draining whilst the pull is motivating and invigorating. Even when the actions include some aspects that we would consider hard work (like going to the gym, changing our dietary routine or going for a long walk), the constant positive visual reminders we set for ourselves tend to override the negative associations we have with the nature of the task or action.

Here are some sample questions we can consider in this section – let's think about how we can answer these to provide the basis for action:

What activities can I undertake that are inspired by my goals and move me in their direction?

Who can support me in sustaining these actions – to whom can I be accountable?

How can these activities be embedded into my daily life so that they become routine?

Don't forget to add your own questions!

Before we go through the activities on inspired actions, let's take a step back. You may find that you need some help in coming up with the actions and might feel a little stuck. Earlier I mentioned turning to inspiring people and things as a possible source for ideas. Well, there are some actions that we all can take - in order to awaken our imagination and creativity - to come up with things we want to do to meet our aims.

- ***Exercise***

Physical activity (especially with an increase in heart rate) is known to increase the 'feel-good' hormones in our bodies, and in this better feeling state, we are naturally more creative and imaginative. We mentioned before the benefit of making decisions from a place of passion – exercise can help with that. Some people use exercise to clear their heads, shift their focus or increase fitness levels – or all of these reasons and more. And if your goal is losing weight, exercise can be the source of inspiration and the action all in one!

- ***Networking***

Spending time with like-minded people with similar goals and aspirations puts us in a more focused mindset and could provide a source of inspiration for ideas on how we can meet our own goals. The more time we spend with other people in this way, the more regularly we tap into this source of sharing and inspiration and the more we get ideas for ourselves. It gives us a chance to sound out our thoughts and be challenged positively and constructively. This can be a unique source of personal growth and development. Groups like Weight Watchers, Fitbit and more recently Peloton Bike are great examples of how networks and communities help us attain our goals.

- ***Information***

Tapping into various sources of information can be of immense benefit when looking for ideas on the actions we can take. There is a lot of information in the form of books, articles, videos and blogs that we can utilise. They were put out there to assist us, so let's make use of them. Ask people in your networks for sources they use and be open to as many sources as possible – your inspiration could come from the most unlikely sources.

Episode 3.1 – Planning and taking action

> ***"The path to success is to take massive, determined actions." Tony Robbins***

Now that you have a clear focus of the goal, the emotion to match and the visual reminders to provide daily inspiration, it's time to set out the list of actions that need to be put into place. These actions will form the basis of the new routine to be embarked on in the achievement of your goal(s).

We can be inspired to take the necessary steps to meet our goals and lay excellent plans to do so, but we need to be motivated and inspired to take the actions we have decided upon. So it's time to write the list of actions you wish to take and again have them clearly displayed for you so they can be 'in your face' as often as possible. The list could just have one action on it to start with and you could add more as you go along. The important thing is to get going.

> ***"You learn how to cut down trees by cutting them down."***
> ***Bateke Proverb***

There are many ways to do this, so consider the images below as just a few ideas and definitely not exhaustive.

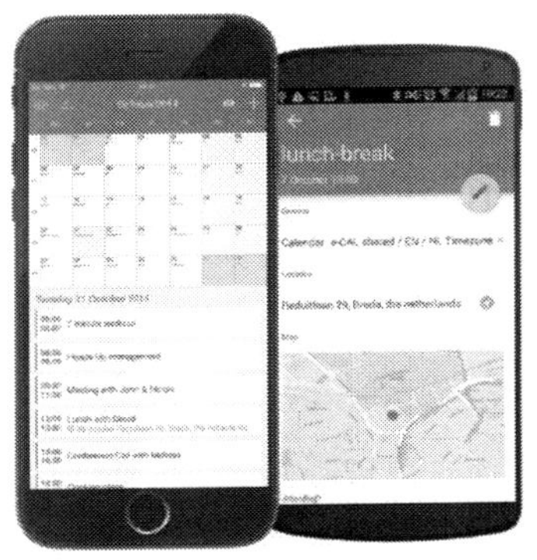

Date: Month Mon - Sun Year

Mon			Fri
Tues			Sat
Wed			Sun
Thurs		Notes:	

CREATE ACTIVITY

Schedule Meeting · Log Call

BASIC

Subject: *

Start Date & Time: *

Duration: *

Status: *

Inbound

Planned

Related to:

Account

Reminders:

1 minute prior
5 minutes prior
10 minutes prior
15 minutes prior
30 minutes prior
2 hours prior
3 hours prior
5 hours prior
1 day prior

Assigned to:

Description:

Behind the scenes tip for setting actions

Actions that hold a degree of pleasure are easier to sustain. Yes, nothing new in that statement, but do we always search for actions that hold some pleasure? Do we recognise the pleasurable aspects of the actions and milk the sensation they bring as often as possible, or do we rather focus on the parts we may not enjoy as much? The more enjoyable the activity, the deeper the emotional connection to it and the quicker and easier the progress.

Pleasure » emotional connection » progress

Example from a teenager

NM is a teenager with autism who came to realise that he wanted to interact more with people outside his immediate family. NM's parents were always the ones interacting with salespeople in shops and he found a way to let them know that he wanted to interact more. They didn't understand what he meant due to his limited vocabulary until the next time they went shopping and NM stepped forward ahead of his parents to speak to the person at the checkout till. He had clearly watched his parents do this and decided what he wanted (realisation), made a decision about what he needed to do to achieve this (planned) and acted on this plan with gusto (action) and clearly enjoyed the process and outcome (pleasure leading to progress)!

Episode 3.2 – Reporting (and recording) our actions

> ***"Accountability is the glue that ties commitment to the result" Bob Proctor***

This is as true in our personal lives as it is in our professional lives. When we are employed, our managers hold us to account to ensure we get the job done. We write reports, feedback on outcomes of projects and meetings and have regular performance reviews. All this to provide the assurance and accountability required to monitor and assess the work we are employed to do. We don't always translate this level of diligence systematically into all areas of our personal lives when it comes to achieving our own goals. But thankfully in some cases we do and here are some examples!

Example from a gym-goer

I started doing an aerobics class in the gym about 3 years ago and at the time there were two or three people in the class that I became friends with. In time, we created a small group on WhatsApp to encourage each other to attend the classes and get the most out of it. In a way, we held each other accountable for attendance and development, and provided motivation to keep it going even when we were quite sore for a couple of days after – at least!

After a while, personal schedules changed, my group buddies and I missed a few classes and our regular attendance as a group reduced. The removal of this source of accountability contributed to a negative effect on my attendance. For those activities where we need it, accountability works to give us the drive to move forward!

And especially in the beginning, it helps sustain the activity.

Example from a keen budding walker

YG took a decision to walk every day but needed a way to maintain her commitment to this goal. She first of all got a Fitbit with mobile phone updates and links. She made the decision to report her activity daily to 2 specific people within her close network who would encourage and motivate her and where necessary, challenge her to do more. That soon went from 2 to 3 and then 4 people! This has kept her on track for many months and put her on the path to achieving her fitness goals.

So what is the activity in this episode? Here are a few things to consider doing at this stage:

- ✓ Choose an accountability buddy (or more than one if you want).
- ✓ Agree a schedule for reporting in activity – daily, 2-3 times a week, or weekly.
- ✓ Agree what kind of feedback you would find helpful – this could be simply acknowledging receipt of reports or discussing how to step up the challenge on a regular basis. For some people this

needs to be 'tough love' with their buddy really pushing them to commit to the actions and report regularly.

- ✓ Decide what would really help YOU and communicate that to your buddy or buddies.

Keeping a progress record

You may choose to do this as part of your gratitude journal and over time, have the pleasure of looking back to see how far you have come on your journey – an effective motivator! Or you may want to keep a weekly achievement record separately. Alternatively, you may be happy the records you have so far on your post-it notes, noticeboards and planners (and on your electronic devices) hold enough information for you at this time. "What's good for you is good," as my yoga teacher Emma often says!

> BEST ME CHECK!
>
> How do my inspired actions reflect the BEST ME?

Make That Switch – Season 4, 'Reinforcement'

> ***"It's not what happens to you that determines how far you go in life. It's how you handle what happens to you." Karen Salmansohn***

In every project or new process that we undertake, there is an instance or a period (or even several) when a dip is experienced. The dip can be a feeling of frustration in the speed of progress, doubt in our ability to achieve the goal, a bad day or week or anything else that stops us or reduces our momentum. This is not at all unusual and gives us the opportunity to reinforce our intentions to reach our original goals or take a pause to redefine or modify any aspect of the process so far.

If we anticipate these instances and plan our response proactively, we are more likely to bounce back into the rhythm we desire easier and quicker. The four episodes in this season give us an idea of how to bounce back and make us aware of the tools to have in our reserve to provide reinforcement.

Let's list some of the possible reasons for the lows we experience.

Slow down or halt in progress

- ✓ Withdrawal of external stimulus (for instance from a motivator)
- ✓ Lack of motivation
- ✓ Self-doubt
- ✓ Uncertainty about the goal

There are most certainly more, but let's focus on what we can do about them.

Episode 4.1 - Emotional reconnection

"Life's challenges are not supposed to paralyze you, they're supposed to help you discover who you are."
Bernice Johnson Reagon

The first thing to keep in mind is the need to consider how we view the lows we experience. Lows can be seen as challenges which hold power to destroy us, or opportunities for us to build and grow in ourselves and our circumstances. If we see them predominantly as the former, we are likely to focus more on the perceived power they hold and introduce the negative mindset we were trying to replace in the first place. However, if we see them as the latter, we already have a mindset that is solution and opportunity-focused, and therefore spend more time, energy and focus seeking out and working on ways to develop and improve and thus, overcome the challenge.

So here is the question to consider in this activity (remember to add any of your own which follow the same idea):

Question

How can I find the emotional connection to my goals and ambitions that allows me to turn lows into highs?

Earlier we looked at the importance and role of positive emotion in the achievement of our goals and especially the added momentum these emotions provide. In periods of lows where we somehow find our focus shifting back to or towards the current, or should I now say previous unwanted situation, our emotions can easily follow this focus, taking us back to the lower end of the emotional scale. To prevent this result, we need a practical and enforceable way of reigniting the positive emotional response we have set for our new selves. What we need is a distracting habit.

It may come as a surprise to you, but this is something that most of us do all the time. In our day to day lives, we find ways of regaining the positive emotions by turning to different and more accessible positive thoughts to distract us from the negative and unwanted stuff. We look for things that make us feel good, like spending time with people we love, going for walks, out to dinner or anything else that we consider a hobby or a pick-me-up. These activities generally return us to, or close to, the way we want to feel by changing the focus of our thoughts and directly influencing our emotions. When we are doing something we enjoy, the emotions of joy and pleasure lead our thoughts to become more positive and generally more pleasant. A really good idea is finding something that makes us laugh! I make it a habit to find something to make me laugh every day, be it a television show, a telephone call to someone I know I can share a good laugh with or something on the internet.

Take a look at the thoughts-emotions map below:

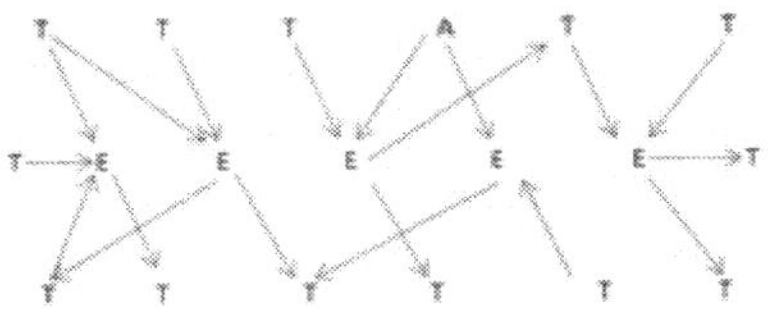

The thought-emotion map - using emotions to reignite momentum

The purpose of this illustration is to point out that the same emotion can be derived from different thoughts and vice versa. We can achieve an emotion to match the one we intend to hold by turning to a different positive thought, or an uplifting action in our times of challenges or lows. The activity of this episode is about seeking out those things that would lead us back to the emotions we desire.

Sometimes, when I find a good feeling thought, I milk it as much as I can by reaching for even better ones. The simple question 'what's better than this?' helps put me into an upward spiral! We often talk about downward emotional spirals that can occur when in periods of depression. So if there can be a downward spiral, why can't there be an upward one?

Consider this example of an upward spiral: I absolutely love admiring the sky on a beautiful day (or even just imagining one) and it makes me feel good. So if I choose to turn to this source of pleasure to get me uplifted, I can imagine a bright blue sky. Asking the question ‘what's better (WB)?’ repeatedly leads me to the following series of images:

• Bright blue sky (BBS) - WB?
• Big fluffy clouds (BFC) in a BBS - WB?

- Bright yellow sun (BYS) shining on BFC in BBS - WB?
- Huge beams of light coming from BYS shining on BFC in BBS

The more beautiful my image the stronger the emotion and the higher up the spiral I go. I've chosen this simple example to use just to demonstrate the concept of upward spiralling. In our imagination, we can apply this to any area of our lives we choose. What would a good day at work look like and what would look even better? What would good health look like and what would be better?

You may have noticed a letter A stuck in the middle of the thoughts-emotions map and wondered why it is there. Well, it certainly wasn't a mistake and the A stands for ACTION! Another way to reignite the positive emotions is to do something active towards your goal. Feeling low and disconnected? The momentum generated from taking action can re-fuel the emotional connection that puts you back on track.

So now it's time to write again and this time, I would suggest a list of activities and thoughts (including memories) that are a source of pleasure or joy for you to form your distracting habit. One such activity may be to refer back to the items you have been writing in your gratitude journal to remind yourself of the positive aspects in your life experience. Write as many activities as you can think of to give yourself as many sources of positive emotion as possible.

Episode 4.2 – Replace all negative self-talk

> ***"Talk to yourself like you would to someone you love." Brene Brown***

If there is one thing a lot of people are good at, it is self-deprecation. And not just for comedic effect! It is not unusual for this to be considered normal and "keeping it real", but in time, it can become engrained, taking a seat at the high table of your mind and is very unlikely to generate the positive emotional connection that we need to progress towards our positive image.

This negative self-talk is not only used in conversations with others, but often self-directed, even within our thoughts. These thoughts then emerge from time to time in unplanned and subtle ways; for instance, when compliments are paid. How often do we find a counterpoint to the praise we receive from others? "You look good in that outfit today" gets the response "it's just an old one I've had for ages" or credit for a piece of work well done gets a response that plays down our own achievement or role that actually led or contributed to the success.

Recently, I remarked to a friend that we are very good at showering our children and young people with compliments and words of encouragement but not as good at doing that with other adults and less likely still to use those positively reinforcing words on ourselves. When we do find the most meaningful words of praise and encouragement to gift ourselves with, and use them regularly, we begin to appreciate ourselves more and reap the benefits that come with those gifts. Remember the self-affirmations in episode 1.3? In times of need, consider re-shooting those scenes for yourself.

So for this activity, write down any and all the negative self-talk you are aware of using. This isn't one for the post-it notes, white board or any other method you have used that is clearly visible! We definitely don't want this at the front and centre of our daily consciousness. This can go on any piece of paper using the format below.

When you have done that, consider for a moment that this piece of paper had been handed to you by someone you love and cherish, and think about how you would counter the negative with a positive statement that would support that person change their focus. Write this down in the adjacent column.

NEGATIVE SELF-TALK	**POSITIVE REPLACEMENT**

When you are done, write each positive replacement statement on a post-it note or other preferred option and put *them* somewhere visible.

Example from a budding writer

I go through periods of self-doubt, even in the process of writing this book. One might have thought writing about developing a positive mindset would indicate that the writer has mastered the art of maintaining that mindset at all times without even the smallest space for negativity to creep in. But that is certainly not the case. Doubts about the book's ability to serve the audience it is meant to reach creep in from time to time and it is my job to manage those doubts. This time the statement was *"Who am I to talk about this subject? I'm no expert!"*

I quickly realised that I can appreciate and almost rejoice in those periods of self-doubt because all they represent is another door on my path leading to more discovery. The key to unlocking these new doors lies in me asking the right questions, formulate the best image in response to the questions and with the right emotional connection, inspire the appropriate action.

So here's what I did: I thought about what positive replacement I needed to replace the negative self-talk. So I replaced *"Who am I to talk about this subject? I'm no expert!"* with *"I am a person with a story and a point of view that can impact the lives of others in a unique way."*

And the latter statement now has its place amongst the other prominent post-it notes on my wall!

Every low period presents an opportunity to reveal to ourselves the power we have within us to progress towards our goals, and in some cases, surprises us with even better options and possibilities.

Episode 4.3 – External reinforcement

> ***"Consistent positive reinforcement is the fuel that keeps the fire burning long enough to achieve any change you desire"***
> ***Anonymous***

In episode 3.2, we looked at the importance of reporting our actions to one or more people within our close network, to make use of the power of accountability to sustain those actions. Here, we want to explore the use of these same people and other sources we can turn to for the reinforcement we may need from time to time. This is also an opportunity to review how the accountability reporting is going.

The main difference between this activity and those in episode 3.2 is the fact that this is meant to be utilised on an ad hoc basis when reinforcement is required, especially when we experience lows.

So ask yourself this question:

Question

Who and/or what can support me with the reinforcement I require along the way?

The person(s) filling the role of 'who' from the question above may or may not be the person(s) you are regularly accountable to and may even be a different person for each time depending on what you need them to do. The 'what' can be one of the actions listed earlier, aimed at awakening our creativity and imagination like exercise, networking and making use of information.

This is the only episode where there is no suggestion to write anything down. The knowledge of who or what can support you for reinforcement when required, is for you to have in mind and utilise as and when the need arises.

So instead, spend some time assessing how effective the regular accountability reports are going. Perhaps discuss the experience with your accountability buddy and find out how it is going for them. Is it still effective and beneficial? Does it need to be stepped up or even down in terms of frequency of reporting and level of feedback? This gives your buddy time to air any concerns or just help them and you refocus on the goal.

Example from budding writers

While writing this book (my first), I teamed up with a friend and fellow budding writer and we both found that writing together was like fuelling each other's engines. We met regularly and at those times our writing progressed rapidly and included us bouncing ideas off each other and constructively challenging each other to do more. When we didn't meet for a period of a couple of weeks or more, there was a noticeable slowing to both our progress. One well timed video call put us back on track and reminded us just how much power there is in external reinforcement which supports us to meet our goals.

Episode 4.4 - Reviewing and modifying actions

"Stay committed to your decisions, but stay flexible in your approach." Tony Robbins

---

Regularly reviewing our actions maintains our focus and connection to the goals we are working towards. It enables us to maintain the level of attention we give them. However, we can't ignore the fact that in some cases, a lack of motivation and/or insurmountable obstacles occurs as an indicator that we need to review and possibly revise our actions or the methods we are using to achieve the goals. This could be after all attempts at reinforcement fail to enable us to find and maintain the emotional connection we need as momentum for the actions we have set. It could be that the actions, when undertaken, are not as feasible as we expected them to be when we set them.

Let's start with some questions that may help us take the next step:

Question

Does the goal need to be bigger or even smaller to get momentum going?

Do the actions that were set still apply to the positive image set in the beginning?

Your accountability person can help you by being a sounding board to reinvigorate yourself as you answer these and more questions. Often at events I attend, when speakers get people to do exercises that involve saying their plans out loud, the most common feedback from attendees (me included) is that the act of speaking the plans or goals makes them real and infuses them with energy.

The answers to these questions could lead to a modification of your actions or perhaps just strengthen your resolve to leave them as they are. In any case, this activity is about giving yourself the opportunity to continually evolve your actions as your life experience leads you to discover things about yourself and your environment as you go about your day to day life.

As a parting thought to this activity, consider this quote:

> ***"What you get by achieving your goals is not as important as what you become by achieving your goals." Henry David Thoreau***

BEST ME CHECK!

Do I reinforce and remind myself of the BEST ME often enough?

Make That Switch (what lies beneath) – 'Share and Shine'

Your story is unique to you and has the power to uniquely impact on another

---

Now it's time to take that further step in our *Make That Switch* series and talk about the underpinning thread that runs all along this model. The two activities in this section are meant to be both the result of using the entire model as well as the companion to the other activities.

As you share, you learn and enrich the experience of others. And as you shine in your own individual way, you learn and enrich the experience of others.

Activity – Sharing thread

"A person is a person because of other persons." African Proverb

---

This activity is pretty simple: seek out every opportunity to share with those around you. These opportunities always present themselves in one way or another, and you never know who may need your particular story, your experience, your take on things and your wisdom.

Talking about what you have learned and are learning motivates, invites discussion and questions from others and yourself. The *Make That Switch* model, with its activities and recommendations to write things down, provides the flexibility to share chunks of activity-based learning as you progress through it.

So you may want to encourage someone else to join you on the journey. Who knows, you might be able to provide mutual positive reinforcement for each other if they do.

"We make a living by what we get, but we make a life by what we give." Norman Macewan

---

Activity – Shining thread

"The world is changed by your example, not by your opinion." Paulo Coelho

---

This final activity is not so much a conscious effort to do anything but more an allowing of your newly-budded-branch to blossom and shine through your life experience for the benefit of others. When you begin to reap the fruit of your new mindset, it shows and you outshine!

OutShine!

This can traditionally be defined as being "much better than someone else in a particular area". But I would like to redefine it here to mean shining outwards! Not to shine **more than** those around you but shine **unto** them. We are all unique down to our talents and vision for our lives. No two people in the same profession express themselves exactly the same so by default when you are expressing your unique self to the world you are offering something only you can. You are OutShining!

So, as you shine out in that unique way, you could think of it as sharing your gift for the benefit of all whom you come into contact with or who experience your gift.

> ***"If you think you are too small to make a difference, spend a night with a mosquito." African Proverb***

Go out and Outshine!!!! Let your life story be the beacon to brighten the path of another.

Going further and deeper........

Here are a few texts I referred to within this book and or used for inspiration. I hope they can offer you the same insights and inspiration that I got from reading them and applying their principles.

- The Little Book of Clarity by Jamie Smart (Capstone, 2015)
- A Heart Full of Peace by Joseph Goldstein (Wisdom Publications, 2007)
- A Book of Virtues: Inner Beauty by Brahma Kumaris Publications (2009)
- A Thousand Paths to Peace by David Baird
- The Law of Attraction: The Basics of the Teachings of Abraham by Esther and Jerry Hicks (Hay House, 2006)
- The Master Key System by Charles Haanel
- Ask and it is Given by Esther and Jerry Hicks (Hay House, 2010)

Printed in Great Britain
by Amazon